apdragons
age 3
ll Howell

Teaching Notes

Contents

Introduction

The *Snapdragons* series is a rich mix of different kinds of stories presented as picture books with expertly written text carefully levelled to provide reading practice at each stage in Key Stage 1.

This set of six books at Stage 3 will help to develop the early reading skills that children need to become competent readers. The six simple stories are told in patterned language with a predictable structure, with repetitive patterns to help build stamina. The stories introduce children to early key words as well as useful vocabulary relating to the different contexts. Children are encouraged to develop early reading skills in mapping spoken word to written word.

Four of the stories at Stage 3 are based in familiar settings: the home, the shops, the hospital and the garden. They reflect everyday life and the readers will quickly identify with the family members and recognise their experiences. The set also includes an animal fantasy and a traditional tale from another culture.

The simple plots at Stage 3 allow children to learn how stories develop. Some contain emotional situations, others will provoke discussions about problem-solving. Children are encouraged to look at the illustrations for visual cues to the words in the text, and to find out what is happening in the story. The picture book presentation will also encourage children to tell the story in their own words and develop their oral skills.

How to introduce the books

Before reading the story for guided or independent reading, always read the title and talk about the picture on the cover.

Go through the book together, looking at the pictures and talking about them. If there are context words (listed in the chart on page 4) that are new or unfamiliar, point them out and read them with the children. Read the story to the children, encouraging confident children to join in with you.

This booklet provides prompts and suggestions for using the books in groups and for guided, group and independent activities, matched to text, sentence and word level objectives. There are also separate Guided Reading Cards available for six titles at each stage. Suggestions are also provided for speaking and listening activities, writing activities, and cross-curricular links. You can use these suggestions to follow on from your reading or at another time.

Reading notes are also provided in each book. They can be found on the inside front and back covers of each book. These suggest friendly prompts and activities for parents or carers reading with their children at home.

Reading skills

Stage 3 develops the ability to:

- predict meaning through the continual support of strong picture-cueing and familiar contexts
- locate and use a growing bank of familiar words, letters and letter sounds
- continue writing sentences and simple stories.

Vocabulary chart

Stage 3		
Grandma's Glasses	Years 1 to 2 High Frequency Words	but came good help her his saw that then too your
	Context words	Grandma glasses table pen Grandpa help drawer book Harry comic Megan cushion teddy curtains shoe Scrap sofa bone everyone things
The Singing Bird	Years 1 to 2 High Frequency Words	but did here little live not now once out some then there very
	Context words	sing(ing) bird everyone happy king little cage sad food
New Blue Shoes	Years 1 to 2 High Frequency Words	but did her here last new next put saw so some there too want were will pink yellow red blue
	Context words	shoes Ella small Grandpa shop some next last full choose
Presents for Baby	Years 1 to 2 High Frequency Words	boy came had him home made some took with
	Context words	presents baby days of the week Grandma Grandpa hospital flowers cry chocolates shoes Gran
Melting Snow	Years 1 to 2 High Frequency Words	came down got little make more new our out than want
	Context words	melt(ing) snow snowing snowman everyone head Tom body Joe helped bigger sun smaller rain sad away
A House for Hedgehog	Years 1 to 2 High Frequency Words	but got his house live much new next so then there too tree your
	Context words	hedgehog cold otter wet rabbit squirrel warm mole dark slipped rolled covered leaves best

Curriculum coverage chart

Stage 3	Speaking and listening	Reading	Writing
Grandma's Glasses			
NLS/SLL	T5/Y1T1 1	T3, S4, W10	T9, T10
Scotland	Level A	Level A	Level A
N. Ireland	Activities: a, b, f, g Outcomes: a, b, c, d, e	Activities: b, c Outcomes: b, c, d	Outcomes: c
Wales	Range: 1 Skills: 2, 3, 4	Range: 1, 5, 6 Skills: 1, 2	Range: 2, 3, 7 Skills: 1, 4, 8
The Singing Bird			
NLS/SLL	T7/Y1T1 1, 4	T8, S1, W10	T9
Scotland	Level A	Level A	Level A
N. Ireland	Activities: b, c, e Outcomes: b, d, e	Activities: b, c Outcomes: d, g, k	Outcomes: a, b, c
Wales	Range: 1, 5, 6 Skills: 1, 2, 3, 4, 5	Range: 1, 2, 4, 5, 6 Skills: 1, 2	Range: 2, 3, 7 Skills: 1, 3, 4
New Blue Shoes			
NLS/SLL	T5/Y1T1 4	T2, S5, W9, W11	T9
Scotland	Level A	Level A	Level A
N. Ireland	Activities: a, b, c, g Outcomes: d	Activities: b, e Outcomes: b, c, f, k	Outcomes: b, c, f
Wales	Range: 1, 5 Skills: 2, 4	Range: 1, 2, 5, 6 Skills: 1, 2	Range: 1, 3, 7 Skills: 1, 2, 3, 8
Presents for Baby			
NLS/SLL	T5/Y1T1 3	T4, S1, S9, W9, W11	T9
Scotland	Level A	Level A	Level A
N. Ireland	Activities: a, f, g Outcomes: a, b, c, e	Activities: a, b Outcomes: b, c, e, f	Outcomes: b, c, f
Wales	Range: 1 Skills: 2, 3	Range: 1, 2, 5 Skills: 1, 2	Range: 2, 3, 7 Skills: 1, 3, 4, 8
Melting Snow			
NLS/SLL	T5/Y1T1 1	T3, S6, S7, W10	T10
Scotland	Level A	Level A	Level A
N. Ireland	Activities: a, f, g Outcomes: a, b, d, e	Activities: a, b, c Outcomes: b, c, d, e, f	Outcomes: b, c
Wales	Range: 1 Skills: 2, 3	Range: 1, 2, 5, 6 Skills: 1, 2	Range: 1, 2, 3 Skills: 1, 3
A House for Hedgehog			
NLS/SLL	T7/Y1T1 4	T3, T7, S1, S4, W2, W12	T11
Scotland	Level A	Level A	Level A
N. Ireland	Activities: a, b, c Outcomes: b, c, d	Activities: a, b, c Outcomes: b, c, d, f	Outcomes: b, c, f, h
Wales	Range: 5, 6 Skills: 1, 2	Range: 1, 2, 5, 6 Skills: 1, 2	Range: 1, 3, 7 Skills: 1, 3, 7, 8

Grandma's Glasses

Reading the story

Introducing the story

- Look at the front cover and read the title. Ask the children: *Who are the people in the picture? What are they looking for?*
- Look through the pages, talking about the illustrations. Ask the children to say who the characters are, and to find their names. Ask: *What has Grandma/Grandpa/Harry found?*
- Encourage the children to identify difficult words by matching the illustration with the word on the page (p4 "drawer", p8 "cushion", p10 "curtains").

During reading

- Praise the children when they follow the text with their eyes, and for only pointing when they have difficulty.
- Prompt the children to use the pictures to help them read the interest words.
- Ask the children what the speech bubbles show.
- Ask the children to find the end of each sentence on pages 6, 8, and 10.

Observing Check that the children:

- read the speech bubbles in an expressive tone
- pause at full stops where two sentences are written consecutively.

Group and independent reading activities

Text level work

Range familiar setting/predictable and patterned language

Objective To notice the difference between spoken and written forms through re-telling known stories; compare oral versions with the written text (T3).

You will need word cards with characters' names:
Grandma, Grandpa, Harry, Megan, Mum, Scrap

- Ask individuals to take turns to pick a card and to tell the group what the character did in the story.
- Each member of the group can find the character in the book and compare what the child remembered with the text.

Observing Do the children recall the characters and events? Do they note which characters look "in", "on", "under" and "behind"?

Sentence level work

Objective To write captions and simple sentences, and to re-read, recognising whether or not they make sense, e.g. wrong word order (S4).

You will need the following word cards:
Grandma lost her glasses
They were on her head

- Ask the children to work with a partner. One child arranges the first group of cards to make a sentence; the other child arranges the second group.
- Ask them to swap and read the sentences carefully.

Observing Do the children check for sense before they swap with their partner? Do they read their partner's sentence carefully?

Word level work

Objective To recognise the critical features of words, e.g. length (W10).
You will need pens and whiteboards.

- Ask the children to look through the book and write down a list of all the things the family found.
- Ask the children to write them down in order of length, beginning with the shortest word.

Observing Do the children recognise the length of the words at a glance, or do they count the letters?

Speaking and listening activities

Objectives To describe story settings and incidents and relate them to own experience and that of others (T5); To describe incidents or tell stories from their own experience, in an audible voice (Y1T1 1).

- Ask the children to describe what happened in the story.
- Ask them to take turns to describe how they lost something in their own homes.
- Ask: *Have you found other things while looking for something that was lost?*

Cross-curricular link

Science: ourselves, why people wear glasses, the other senses

Writing

Objectives To write about events in personal experience linked to a variety of familiar incidents from stories (T9); To use patterned stories as models for their own writing (T10).

You will need the following sentences written on the board, or on paper for each child:
Grandma looked…the table and she saw her…
Grandpa looked…the drawer and he found his…

- Demonstrate writing a sentence from the story by filling in the gaps in the sentence.
- Point out that in the story the characters look in, under or behind things.
- Ask the children to fill in the missing words in the two sentences, using the story as a model.
- Ask them to write their own third sentence about themselves, and choose a preposition to use.

The Singing Bird

Reading the story

Introducing the story

- Look at the front cover and read the title. Discuss the illustration with the children and ask them to suggest where the story might be set.
- Read the text on page 2 to the children, and then look through the pages, talking about what happens in the illustrations.
- Point out the text on page 13. Ask the children to say where they should begin reading it.

During reading

- Praise the children when they follow the text with their eyes, and for only pointing when they have difficulty.
- Prompt the children to use the pictures to help them read the interest words.
- On page 5, ask the children to find the punctuation that shows when someone is speaking and to read the words in between.
- On page 13, ask: *Why are the words written in an upwards curve?* (To match the way the little bird is flying up into the sky.)

Observing Check that the children:

- read the high frequency words on sight
- read the text on page 13 in the right direction
- understand why the king set the bird free.

Group and independent reading activities

Text level work

Range traditional/from another culture/predictable and patterned language

Objective To notice the difference between spoken and written forms through re-telling known stories; compare oral versions with the written text (T3).

- Ask the children if they have heard any similar stories, such as "The Emperor and the Nightingale".
- Explain that when traditional tales were first made up they were not written down. They were told instead, so there were often many different versions.
- Ask the children to work with a partner and to tell each other the story of "The Singing Bird".
- Ask them to check their re-telling with the book to see how their version differed from the text.

Observing Do the children use story language and recall the order of events in the story?

Sentence level work

Objective To expect written text to make sense and to check for sense if it does not (S1).

You will need sets of the following sentences written on strips of card:
There was once a little bird.
The king said, "Come and live in this cage."
The little bird was sad.
Then the king let the bird out.
Everyone was happy.

- Give the children a set of mixed-up sentence cards. Ask them to read the sentences and put them into order.

Observing Do the children read all the sentences before putting them into order? Do they check the order by looking in the book?

Word level work

Objective To recognise the critical features of words, e.g. words within words (W10).

- Ask the children to read the text on page 2 and find the longest word. (everyone)

- Ask them to look through the text to find the word again. (p14)
- Ask the children to think of other words that are made in the same way, e.g. someone, somebody.

Observing Do the children think of words beginning with "some" or ending with "one"?

Speaking and listening activities

Objectives To re-enact stories in a variety of ways, e.g. through role-play (T7); To describe incidents or tell stories from their own experience, in an audible voice (Y1T1 1); To explore familiar themes and characters through improvisation and role-play (Y1T1 4).

- Choose children to sit in the hot seat.
- Ask the child in the hot seat to choose to be either the king or the little bird.
- Ask them to describe what happened to them in the story. Encourage the other children to ask them questions.

Cross-curricular links

PSHE: living things have needs; what harms local and natural environments
Science: life processes and living things

Writing

Objective To write about events in personal experience linked to a variety of familiar incidents in stories (T9).

- Ask the children to suggest other animals that someone might keep. (e.g. a butterfly)
- Choose one of the children's suggestions and write two opening sentences for a new story. (e.g. "There was once a little butterfly. She flew in the sun.")
- Give the children the beginning of two more sentences. (e.g. "I kept her in…" "She was …"). Ask them to finish the sentences and write one more to finish the story.

New Blue Shoes

Reading the story

Introducing the story

- Look at the front cover and read the title. Discuss the illustration with the children and ask them to suggest where the story might be set.
- Look through the pages, talking about what happens in the illustrations, and confirm the settings. (shoe shops)
- Ask the children to identify the colours in the pictures and find the words on the pages.

During reading

- Praise the children when they follow the text with their eyes, and for only pointing when they have difficulty.
- On pages 2 and 3, ask the children: *What is wrong with the blue shoes?* Ask them to find the word "small" on these pages.
- On page 4, ask: *Where are the words spoken by Ella?* Ask the children to put one finger on the punctuation marks that show where she begins speaking, and another finger at the end of the speech. Ask the children to read the words in between the speech marks. Ask them to find the end of this sentence. Ask: *How do you know this is the end?*

Observing Check that the children:

- read the colour words on sight
- understand the function of speech marks and full stops
- interpret the illustrations to help them understand the story.

Group and independent reading activities

Text level work

Range familiar setting/predictable language/repetitive patterns

Objective To use phonological, contextual, grammatical and graphic knowledge to work out, predict and check the meanings of unfamiliar words and to make sense of what they read (T2).

You will need coloured cards, counters or cubes (blue, yellow, pink, red), pens and whiteboards.

- Give the children a set of the four colours.
- Ask the children to find the colours in the book, to find the word for each colour and to write it on their whiteboards.

Observing Do the children use their knowledge of initial sounds to find the words?

Sentence level work

Objective To recognise capital letters when reading, and name them correctly (S5).

- Ask the children to look through the pages of the book and identify the words with capital letters.
- Talk about how sentences and names always begin with capital letters.
- Ask the children to find a word that is written using only capital letters. (p14 "FULL")
- Ask: *Why do you think this word has been written in this way?*

Observing Do the children understand the uses of capital letters? Do they read "FULL" on page 14 with emphasis?

Word level work

Objectives To read on sight high frequency words for Y1 (W9); To spell common irregular words from Appendix List 1 (W11).

- Ask the children to look through the text from pages 2 to 9, and to write down the words that begin with "s". (shoes, small, said, some, shop, so, saw)
- Ask them to practise spelling the words using Look, Cover, Write and Check.
- Hold a quick spelling test.

Observing Do the children spell the high frequency words correctly? (said, some, so, saw)

Speaking and listening activities

Objectives To describe story settings and incidents and relate them to own experience and that of others (T5); To explore familiar themes and characters through improvisation and role-play (Y1T1 4).

- Set up a shoe shop in the play corner.
- Encourage the children to take turns to be the shopkeeper and a person buying new shoes.

Cross-curricular link

Numeracy: pairing, counting in twos (how many pairs of shoes are there in the group or class?)

Writing

Objective To write about events in personal experience linked to a variety of familiar incidents from stories (T9).

- Write the beginning of this sentence on the board: "My shoes are...".
- Ask the children to finish the sentence by adding the colour of their shoes, and to illustrate it using the right colour.

Presents for Baby

Reading the story

Introducing the story

- Look at the front cover and read the title. Ask the children: *What is the child in the picture doing?*
- Look through the pages, talking about what happens in the illustrations.
- Ask the children to identify the days of the week on each page.
- Identify any unfamiliar interest words with the children, e.g. p2 "hospital", p4 "flowers", p9 "chocolates".

During reading

- Praise the children when they follow the text with their eyes, and for only pointing when they have difficulty.
- On pages 2 and 3, ask the children to look at the illustration and say where Mum is going. Ask: *Can you find the word "hospital"?*
- There are two sentences in the text boxes. Ask the children to show you where the first sentence ends and the second one begins.
- Ask: *What day of the week is written on the page?* Ask them to show you where it is.
- Encourage the children to read the speech bubbles with expression.

Observing Check that the children:

- read the high frequency words on sight
- use the term "sentence" and identify the full stops
- find the days of the week twice.

Group and independent reading activities

Text level work

Range familiar setting/predictable and patterned language

Objective To read familiar, simple stories independently, to point while reading and make correspondence between words said and words read (T4).

You will need word cards for the days of the week.

- Ask the children to work with a partner.
- Ask them to take turns to choose a day of the week. Their partner finds the page in the book for that day, and reads the text.

Observing Do the children find the page by using the order of the days of the week?

Sentence level work

Objective To expect written text to make sense and to check for sense if it does not (S1); To use a capital letter for the start of a sentence (S9).

You will need the following sentences written on word cards:
On Monday, Mum went to hospital.
On Tuesday, Mum had a baby boy.
On Wednesday, I went to see Mum and the baby.

- Remind the children about the uses of capital letters. Explain that capital letters are used at the start of sentences. They are only used in the middle of sentences for names.
- Ask the children to put the word cards into order so that they make sense.

Observing Do the children understand that the word "On" must start the sentence because it has a capital letter?

Word level work

Objectives To read on sight high frequency words for Y1 (W9); To spell common irregular words from Appendix List 1 (W11).

- Write the following four-letter words from the story on the board: "came", "took", "some", "made", "home".
- Ask the children to look through the text and find each word, and note how many times it occurs.
- Ask them to write the words and use Look, Cover, Write and Check to practise their spelling. Hold a quick spelling test.

Observing Do the children find the words quickly and easily, scanning the lines of text?

Speaking and listening activities

Objectives To describe story settings and incidents and relate them to own experience and that of others (T5); To ask and answer questions, make relevant contributions, offer suggestions and take turns (Y1T1 3).

- Ask the children to imagine they have a new baby brother or sister.
- Ask: *What would you take as a present for the baby? Why?*

Cross-curricular link

PSHE: belonging to various groups and communities such as family and school

Writing

Objective To write about events in personal experience linked to a variety of familiar incidents in stories (T9).

- Discuss with the children what they do on the different days of the week.
- Demonstrate how to write some of their suggestions on the board, using the text as a model, e.g. "On Monday,...".
- Over the course of a week, ask the children to write one sentence about what they did each day.

Melting Snow

Reading the story

Introducing the story

- Look at the front cover and read the title. Ask the children: *What do you think this story will be about?*
- Look through the pages, talking about what happens in the illustrations.
- Ask the children to find the words "bigger and bigger" on page 6. Ask them to find the words "smaller and smaller" on page 9. Ask: *Why do you think these words are written in this way?*

During reading

- Prompt the children to use the illustrations to help them work out difficult words.
- Encourage the children to use the punctuation to help them make sense of the text, re-reading where a sentence runs on two or three lines.

Observing Check that the children:

- use more than one strategy to make sense of what they read
- understand the effect of the different sizes of print.

Group and independent reading activities

Text level work

Range familiar setting/predictable language/repetitive patterns

Objective To notice the difference between spoken and written forms through re-telling known stories (T3).

You will need the following word cards:
head, body, rain, sun, snow, sad

- Ask the children to work with a partner and take turns to pick a word card.

- Ask them to find the word in the text and to re-tell the part of the story where the word features using their own words.

Observing Do the children scan the text to find the words on the page? Do they need to read the text to recall what happened?

Sentence level work

Objectives To begin using the term "sentence" to identify sentences in text (S6); to know that a line of writing is not necessarily the same as a sentence (S7).

- Ask the children to turn to page 12. Ask them to read the two lines of text and find the beginning and end of the sentences. Ask: *How many sentences are there on the page?*
- Ask the children to turn to page 3. Ask them to read the two lines of text. Ask: *How many sentences are there on this page?*
- Ask them to read the story again and find sentences that are written on two lines. Say: *Now find a sentence that is written on three lines.*

Observing Do the children look for capital letters and full stops to identify complete sentences?

Word level work

Objective To recognise the critical features of words, e.g. words within words (W10).

You will need pens and whiteboards

- Write "snowman" on the board. Point out that it is made from two smaller words, "snow" and "man".
- Ask the children to suggest other words that could be made in a similar way, beginning with "snow" and ending with another word, e.g. flake, ball, drift, drop. Write these words as a separate list.
- Ask them to write complete words on their whiteboards by combining "snow" with words from the list.

- Encourage the children to look through the story and find another word made from two smaller words. (everyone, snowmen)

Observing Do the children combine two smaller words without putting a space between them?

Speaking and listening activities

Objectives To describe story settings and incidents and relate them to own experience and that of others (T5); To describe incidents or tell stories from their own experience, in an audible voice (Y1T1 1).

- Ask the children to think about how to make a snowman.
- Ask them to take turns to describe each step, using words to show a process, e.g. first, next, then.
- Prompt the children to add details, e.g. eyes, nose, hat.

Cross-curricular link
Science: materials and their properties, freezing and melting

Writing

Objective To use patterned stories as models for their own writing (T10).

- Ask the children to find the words "bigger" and "smaller" in the story.
- Explain that the way the words are written matches their meaning.
- Model writing two sentences on the board, e.g. "This snowman is bigger." "This snowman is smaller."
- Ask them to draw their own big and small snowmen, and then to write a sentence for each, making the size of the words match their meaning.

A House for Hedgehog

Reading the story

Introducing the story

- Look at the front cover and read the title. Ask the children to find Hedgehog in the picture and point to the word in the title.
- Ask the children to look through the book and find the names of the animals.
- Ask: Where is the beginning and ending? Look at the picture on page 2 again. Ask: *What is different about the last picture?* (Hedgehog is happy in the last picture.)

During reading

- Praise the children when they follow the text with their eyes, and for only pointing when they have difficulty.
- Prompt the children to use the pictures to help them read the interest words.
- Praise children who read the dialogue in an expressive tone.
- On page 3, ask them to find the punctuation that shows when someone is speaking and read the words in between.

Observing Check that the children:

- read the high frequency words on sight
- take note of speech punctuation
- understand why Hedgehog now likes his own house.

Group and independent reading activities

Text level work

Range fantasy/predictable and patterned language

Objectives To notice the difference between spoken and written forms through re-telling known stories; compare oral versions with written text (T3); To re-enact stories in a variety of ways, e.g. through role-play (T7).

- Ask the children to look through the text and find where speech is written.
- Ask children to take turns to be Hedgehog, and others to take the parts of the other characters.
- Ask them to read the book again, each reading only the words that are spoken by their character.
- Discuss what is missing from the story. Ask: *If we were to act the story as a play, what could we do to fill in the missing parts?*

Observing Do the children notice that the descriptions of Hedgehog's actions are missing from their reading?

Sentence level work

Objectives To expect written text to make sense and to check for sense if it does not (S1); To write captions and simple sentences, and re-read, recognising whether or not they make sense (S4).

- Discuss why Hedgehog went looking for a new house with the children.
- Model how to write a sentence about Hedgehog's house, e.g. "Hedgehog's house is too cold."
- Ask the children to choose one of the other animals' houses, to draw a picture of it, and to write a sentence about why Hedgehog did not want to live there.
- Prompt the children to find the page in the text, check that what they have written makes sense, and to correct their sentence if necessary.

Observing Do the children use capital letters and full stops?

Word level work

Objectives To practise and secure alphabetic letter knowledge and alphabetic order (W2); To learn new words from reading and shared experiences, and to make collections of personal interest or significant words and words linked to particular topics (W12).

- Ask the children to look through the story and write a list of the animals that feature in it. (Hedgehog, Otter, Rabbit, Squirrel, Mole)
- Ask them to practise spelling these words using Look, Cover, Write and Check.
- Ask the children to write the list in alphabetical order.

Observing Do the children scan the words to find the animal names?

Speaking and listening activities

Objectives To re-enact stories in a variety of ways, e.g. through role-play (T7); To explore familiar themes and characters through improvisation and role-play (Y1T1 4).

- Ask the children to take turns to play the part of Hedgehog. The others in the group take the parts of the other animals.
- Ask them to act out the story in their own words and to imitate how the animals move.
- Encourage the children to add to the dialogue.
- Ask some of the groups to perform their plays.

Cross-curricular links
Citizenship: animals and us
D&T: homes

Writing

Objective To make simple picture storybooks with sentences, modelling them on basic text conventions (T11).

- Explain that you are going to make a class book about Hedgehog's story.
- Ask the children to revisit the sentences they wrote and corrected about the animals' houses, and re-write them as finished pieces.
- Ask them to suggest a page to finish the book, and to write a sentence for it.

Oxford Reading Tree resources at this level

There is a range of material available at a similar level to these stories which can be used for consolidation or extension.

Stage 3

Teacher support

- Teacher's Handbook
- Flopover Book
- Big Book for Stage 3 Stories
- Guided Reading Cards for Stage 3 Stories
- Take-Home Card for each story
- Extended Stories
- Storytapes / More Storytapes
- Context Cards
- Workbooks 3a and 3b
- Sequencing Cards Photocopy Masters
- Group Activity Sheets Book 1 Stages 1–3
- ORT Games Stages 1–3
- Woodpeckers Introductory Phonic Workbooks A & B

Further reading

- Oxford Reading Tree Storybooks for Core Reading
- Fireflies Non-Fiction
- Fact FinderS Units A and B
- Glow-worms Poetry

Electronic

- Clip Art
- Stage 3 Talking Stories
- ORT Online www.OxfordReadingTree.com
- Floppy and Friends

For introducing phonics

- First Phonics Stage 3

For developing phonological awareness

- Alphabet frieze, Tabletop Alphabet Mats, Alphabet Photocopy Masters
- Card Games
- First Story Rhymes

OXFORD
UNIVERSITY PRESS

Great Clarendon Street, Oxford OX2 6DP

Oxford University Press is a department of the University of Oxford. It furthers the University's objective of excellence in research, scholarship, and education by publishing worldwide in

Oxford New York

Auckland Bangkok Buenos Aires Cape Town Chennai Dar es Salaam Delhi Hong Kong Istanbul Karachi Kolkata Kuala Lumpur Madrid Melbourne Mexico City Mumbai Nairobi São Paulo Shanghai Taipei Tokyo Toronto

Oxford is a registered trade mark of Oxford University Press in the UK and in certain other countries

First published 2004

British Library Cataloguing in Publication Data

Data available

Cover illustrations by Lucy Truman

Teacher's Notes: ISBN 0 19 845526 7

10 9 8 7 6 5 4 3 2 1

Page make-up by Fakenham Photosetting, Fakenham, Norfolk

Printed in Great Britain by Ashford Colour Press, Gosport, Hants